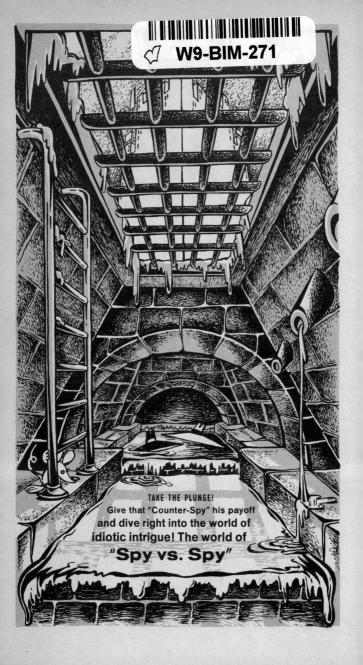

TAKE THE PLUNGE!
Give that "Counter-Spy" his payoff
and dive right into the world of
idiotic intrigue! The world of

"Spy vs. Spy"

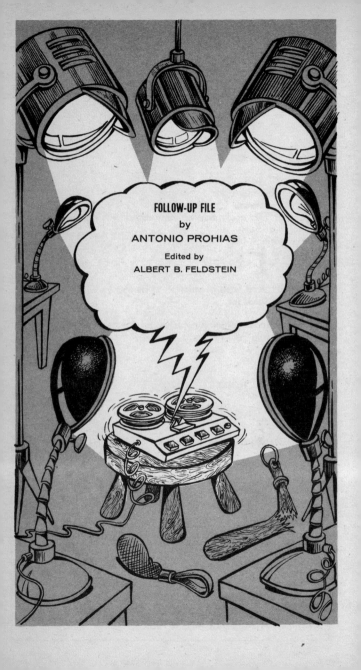

FOLLOW-UP FILE

by

ANTONIO PROHIAS

Edited by

ALBERT B. FELDSTEIN

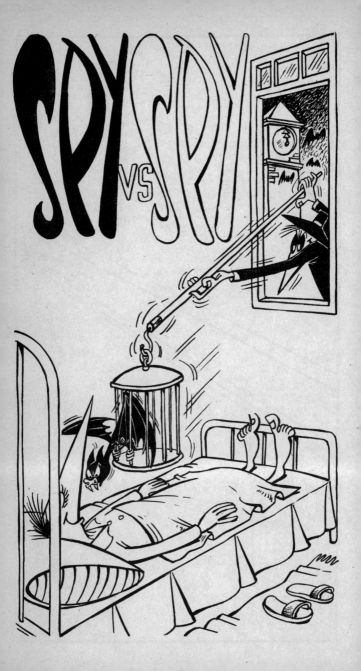

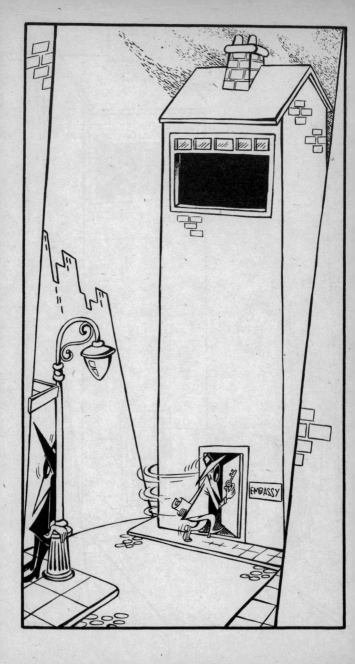

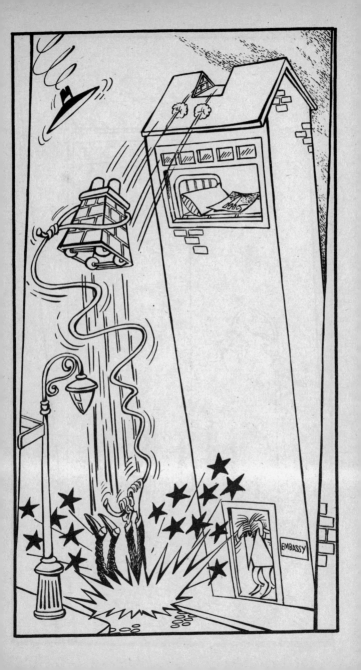

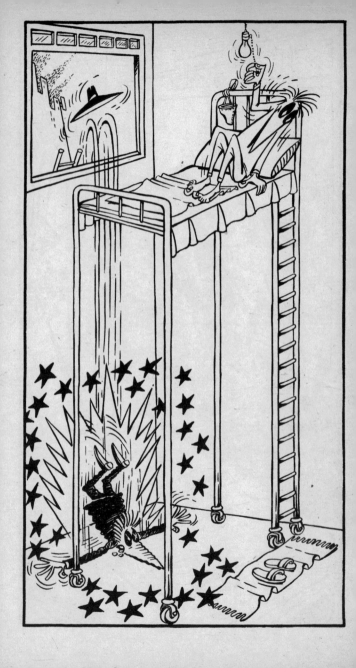

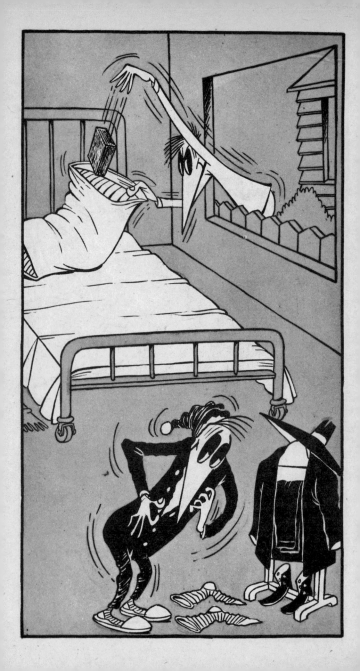

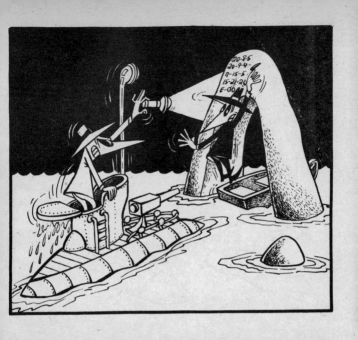

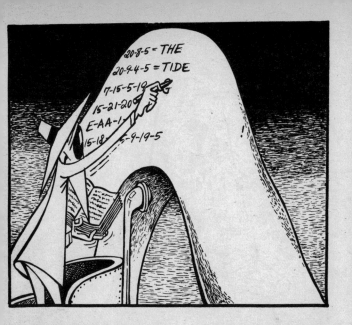

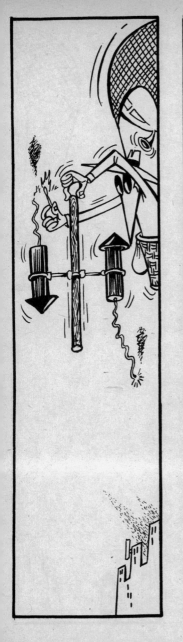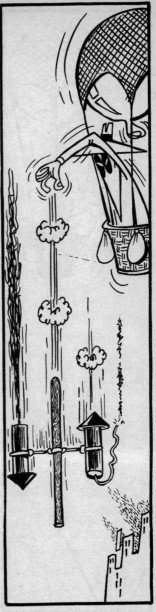

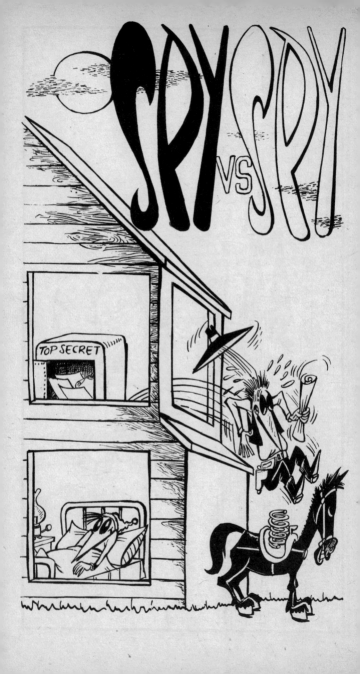

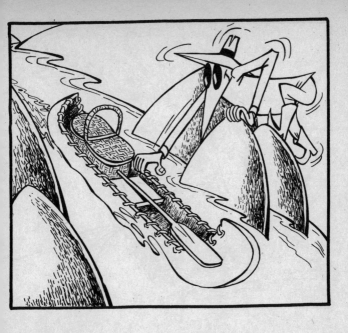

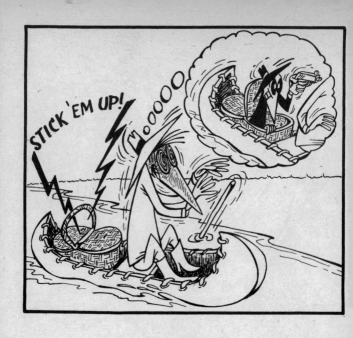

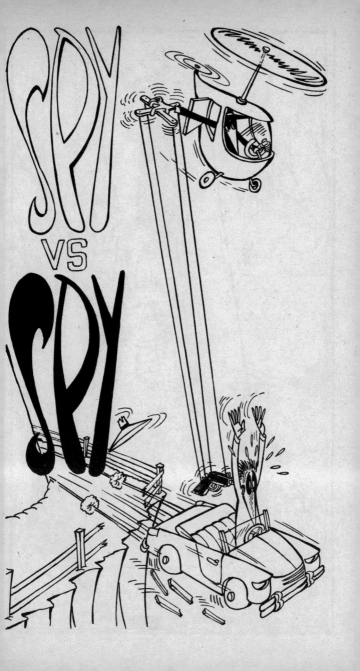

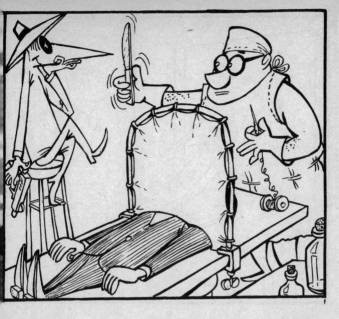

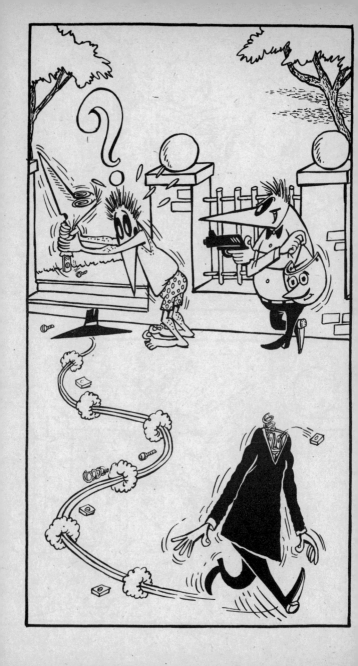

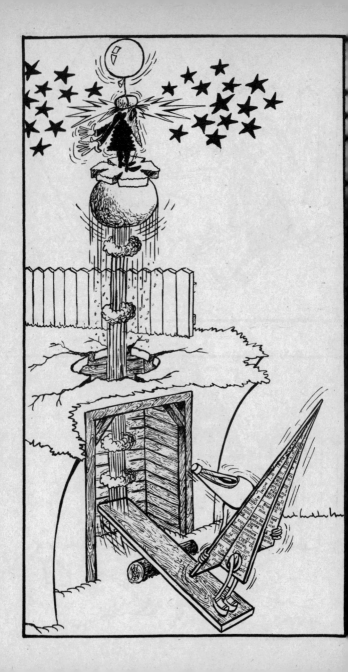

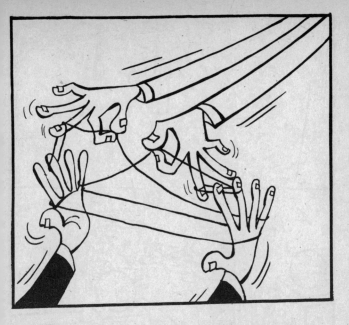

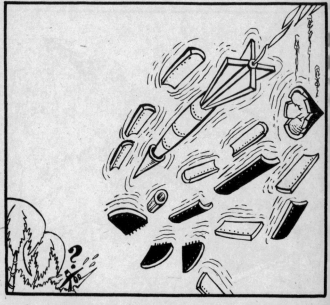

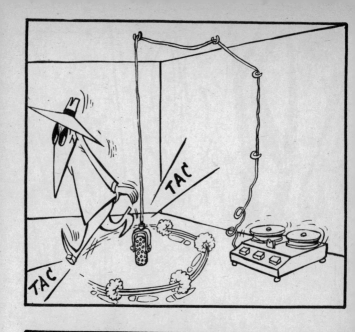

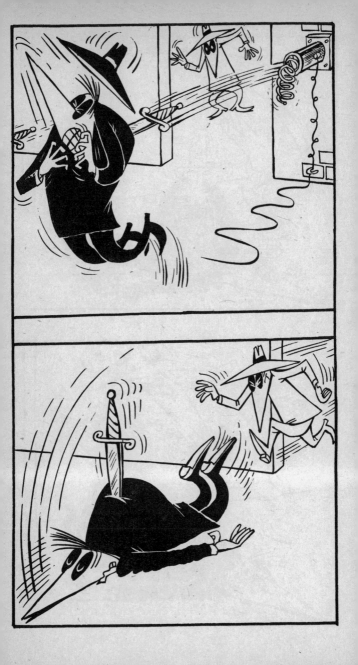

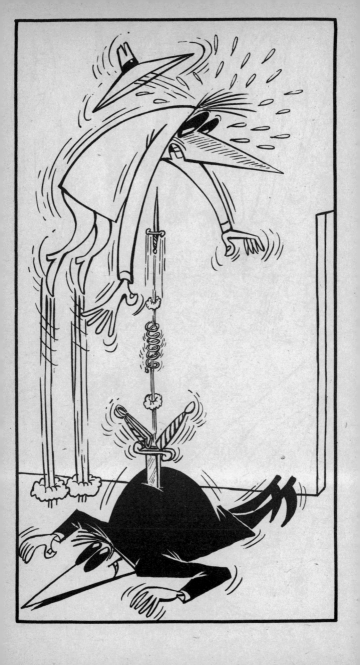

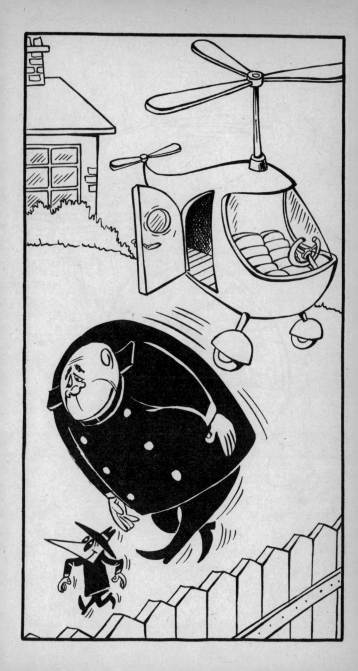

MAIL COLLECTION
11.00 P.M.

TICK TICK